HOW TO
HANDLE STRESS
by Don Warrick

NAVPRESS ●®

A MINISTRY OF THE NAVIGATORS
P.O. BOX 6000, COLORADO SPRINGS, COLORADO 80934

© 1989 by Don Warrick
All rights reserved, including translation
ISBN 08910-95284

Unless otherwise identified, all Scripture quota-
tions in this publication are from the *New King
James Version* (NKJV), Copyright © 1979, 1980,
1982, Thomas Nelson, Inc., Publishers.

Printed in the United States of America

HOW TO HANDLE STRESS

Stress is an important issue in your life! It can result in a defeated life, robbed of the joy God intended and controlled by circumstances. However, stress can also bring victorious living regardless of our circumstances and become a source of growth, strength, and most importantly, developing an intimate relationship with Jesus Christ. The Scriptures offer great hope, insight, and even blessings for those who are willing to learn and obey God's principles for handling stress and trials.

Stress Is a Spiritual Issue

The way we manage stress reveals the genuineness (1 Peter 1:6-7) and maturity (Genesis 22:1-18) of our faith and our understanding of who our Lord is and how He uses trials (2 Corinthians 4:8-18). It reflects the condition of our heart and our relationship with Jesus Christ. Our Lord uses stressful situations so we can be "conformed to the image of His Son" (Romans 8:29) and "Draw near to God" (James 4:8).

Hope For Stressed Christians

Christians will have trials (John 16:33) but will also be given the resources and strength to gain victory (2 Corinthians 12:9-10). The Bible shows us how we can actually rejoice and glory in our tribulations, knowing that they will produce patience, perfect and complete us, and develop perseverance, character, and hope (Romans 5:3-4, James 1:2-4). We are even promised that "all things work together for good to those who love God, to those who are the called according to His purpose" (Romans 8:28), and that we will receive blessings from facing trials in God's strength (Matthew 5:11-12).

God shows great compassion for those struggling with difficulties, large or small, and patiently waits for us to come to Him and rely on His strength rather than our own. In Matthew 11:28, Jesus says, "Come to Me, all you who labor and are heavy laden, and I will give you rest." Almost every example we have in the Bible of God's saints is of people facing difficult and highly stressful circumstances. Imagine Daniel about to face a lion's den or Shadrach, Meshach, and Abed-Nego about to be cast into a fiery furnace. Consider Paul singing praises to God and witnessing as he sat chained in prison with fresh stripes on his back.

When you think your burdens are too great to bear and need hope in time of stress, remember Jesus, who gave up His position, came in the likeness of men in the form of a servant, and suffered as no man has ever suffered that we might have eternal life (Philippians 2:5-8). Jesus understands suffering and trials. Luke 22:41-46 says that Jesus was in such agony that His sweat became like great drops of blood falling down to the ground.

What Is Stress?

While the term *stress* is not found in Scripture, the Bible does use the term *distress* and tells us how to be victorious in trials. *Distress* is used throughout the Bible to describe people feeling anguished because of difficulties. It is first used in Genesis 35:3 when Jacob speaks of God who "answered me in the day of my distress."

Stress is our mental, emotional, physical, and behavioral response to anxiety-producing events. Anxiety-producing events are called "stressors" and include frustrating circumstances, time pressures, family and other relational problems, financial difficulties, disappointments, heartbreaking circumstances, physical problems, and other situations that result in strain, pressure, or tension.

Stress begins mentally when we consciously or subconsciously "perceive" something as stressful. This is significant. Positive thinkers simply do not perceive most circumstances as stressful, so they automatically eliminate most of their stress! A person who dwells on negative thoughts turns most circumstances—good or bad, important or unimportant—into stress. The Bible tells us to meditate on praiseworthy things (Philippians 4:8) and points out that "for as he thinks in his heart, so is he" (Proverbs 23:7). Stress is a disease of the heart. It is not circumstances, but rather how we perceive circumstances based on what is in our heart, that causes stress. This is why some are joyful in the worst of circumstances and others complain in circumstances that many would find enviable.

Our *emotional* response to stress depends primarily on our mental response and our emotional maturity. While some feelings are physiologically based, most can be traced to what we have been thinking about or exposing our mind to. Depression, for example, is primarily induced by dwelling on negative thoughts. The way we process and express our emotions increases or decreases stress and affects our emotional development and maturity. Those who never learn to rule their emotions live in bondage to circumstances and feelings. Proverbs 25:28 says, "Whoever has no rule over his own spirit is like a city broken down, without walls." The Bible never suggests that we should be spared from struggling with stressful emotional issues. God uses our struggles to teach us how to handle failure, disappointments, anger, frustration, sorrow, and grief. Emotional immaturity destines us to being victims of stress and causes of stress for others.

Our *physical* response to stress can affect our nervous system, blood pressure, blood composition, breathing, body chemistry, glandular secretions, muscle reactions, and other body functions. These changes can be helpful or harmful, depending on how we perceive and manage stress and how physically fit our bodies are. Effective stress management frees our physical coping mechanisms to work for us rather than against us.

Behaviorally, we respond to stress by adapting with increased effectiveness and performance or by behaving in erratic, unconstructive, self-defeating ways. For example, mismanaged stress may cause decreased productivity, irritability, an increase in accidents and mistakes, temper tantrums, rebellion, smoking, drinking, overeating, denying reality, and taking our stress out on others.

Understanding Stress

To manage stress effectively, it helps to improve our understanding of stress.

Stress can be positive or negative. The Bible presents many examples of people experiencing victory and peace in extremely stressful circumstances. But improperly managed, stress can have serious consequences.

Stress is relative to: (1) how much we have; (2) how long we have it; and (3) how we manage it. The most critical of the three is how we manage it.

Most stress is self-created. Stress comes from stress-producing circumstances and our own stress-producing behaviors. While we tend to attribute most stress to circumstances, our own behaviors are by far the bigger culprit.

Our coping responses (how we cope with stress) are habits that increase or decrease stress. Habits, good or bad, come from practicing behaviors until they become normal ways to behave. Fortunately, we can significantly improve our ability to manage stress by practicing new, more effective coping responses.

Our coping response has a multiplier effect. We cannot be stressed without stressing others. One "stress carrier" in a home can stress an entire family. Stress carriers spread tension and conflict, cause disharmony and discord, consume time, and become stumbling blocks for others.

Not all stress should be avoided. We naturally try to avoid or escape from trials. However, if we are living in God's will and are experiencing trials or difficult circumstances, we are exactly where we should be! While there is no virtue in self-inflicted trials, we should not avoid situations that God has allowed to train and perfect us. We should also be careful not to protect or rescue others from trials they need for their growth.

Being defeated by stress is a choice! The Bible offers no excuses for being defeated by stress (1 Corinthians 10:13).

Why Christians Have Trials

In this age when salvation is sometimes portrayed as a smooth road to health, wealth, and happiness, some are shaken by the trials and seemingly unexplainable tragedies that Christians encounter. When a small child dies, a crippling disease strikes, or injustice seems to thrive, how do we explain such circumstances in the lives of those who proclaim to love the Lord? There are at least four reasons why Christians experience stress and trials:

Some stressful circumstances come from living in a sinful world that is reaping the natural consequences of living apart from God's laws. Satan's deception and man's folly have created a world out of control.

Most trials are self-created and come from personally living outside of God's laws and will.

Disobedience, self-centeredness, lying, envy, jealousy, laziness, irresponsibility, and immorality, for example, cause stress and may have long-term natural consequences, even though we can be forgiven if we are truly repentant.

Committed Christians live in the world but are not of the world. Christians are strangers in a foreign land and will have tribulations (Acts 14:22), experience suffering (1 Timothy 3:12), and will not be understood or accepted by the world (James 4:4).

Trials are used by God for our training and completion and His purposes and glory.

The Purpose of Trials

Few issues are more important to our spiritual growth than how we respond to trials. Yet Christians often know little about the purpose of trials. Some of God's purposes are to:

Test the genuiness of our faith (1 Peter 4:12-19). We are challenged in 2 Corinthians 13:5, "Examine yourselves as to whether you are in the faith." If we consistently abandon our faith during trials or lack the power to manage them, it is possible we may not be truly saved.

Test the maturity of our faith (1 Peter 5:6-10). The way we handle trials show evidence of our spiritual maturity or immaturity.

Experience God's strength in our weaknesses (2 Corinthians 12:7-10). Paul pleaded to be relieved of his infirmity, but God allowed it to continue to show His strength in Paul's weakness. Trials often strip us of our pride, self-centeredness, focus on worldly pleasures, and confidence in our own resources. They keep us humbly on our knees in a close relationship with our Lord.

Strengthen our faith and keep our hopes on God, not circumstances (Hebrews 11). Trials can deepen our understanding of God and His mercy and power (Romans 8:35-39). We can place our faith in imperfect people and unpredictable circumstances, or in a perfect and unchanging God (Hebrews 13:8).

Build character and perfect and complete us (2 Timothy 2:1-15). It has been said that the true value of a soldier is never known in peace time. Trials reveal the strength of our character and can build the qualities we need to serve and obey the Lord.

Prepare us to help others (2 Corinthians 1:3-4). God comforts us in all our tribulations so we will be able to comfort others. The more we suffer, the more we are able to show mercy and compassion to others in their suffering.

Learn contentment in all circumstances (Philippians 4:11-13). A discontented Christian is always a defeated Christian. Discontentment is a way of voicing our displeasure to God, of telling Him we deserve better than He has allowed us to have.

Teach us to be bold and not fearful (Psalm 27:1-3). If we are living in God's will, nothing can touch us that God does not allow. We have nothing to fear and can live boldly, knowing that God will provide for all of our needs.

Provide a positive witness to others (Acts 20:18-24). The world is much more interested in seeing how Christians handle trials than in how they handle blessings. Trials often result in outreaches we never could have anticipated.

Change our perspective (1 John 2:15-17). Without trials, it is easy to become absorbed in a life of trivial pursuit, making important things of no eternal consequence. Trials tend to reveal how wrapped up in self we really are. When we experience personal suffering or are involved with others who are suffering, our perspective often changes.

Managing Stress

No matter what your circumstances are, how stressed you presently feel, or how badly you have mismanaged stress in the past, the Scriptures show the way to turning difficulties into opportunities and defeats into victories. There are five basic ways you can manage stress:

- Prepare for the battles and challenges of the day.
- Change your stress-producing circumstances.
- Change your stress-producing behaviors.
- Develop an effective coping response based on biblical principles.
- Manage your life according to biblical principles.

In applying these options, the key is to MANAGE STRESS IN THE SPIRIT AND NOT THE FLESH so your efforts are directed by the Holy Spirit rather than self will. Managing stress in the flesh limits us to our own strength and wisdom, results in frustration from our failures or pride from our successes, and forfeits our access to God's power, will, and blessings.

Prepare for the Battles and Challenges of the Day

What do you do to prepare for the battles and challenges of the day? If the answer is "Very little," you may have discovered the major reason you get stressed. An unprepared person in any endeavor is easily defeated. When we are spiritually unprepared, we are easy prey for Satan as he "walks around like a roaring lion seeking whom he may devour" (1 Peter 5:8). Like soldiers going into battle, we are commanded to "put on the whole armor of God, that you may be able to stand against the wiles of the devil" (Ephesians 6:11).

There are several ways we can prepare for the battles and challenges of the day:

Start the day in spiritual balance. Never neglect this important step! Begin each day with a devotion, spending time in prayer, studying the Scriptures, worshiping God, and discovering who the God we serve is. Mark 1:35 says that Jesus rose long before daylight to find a solitary place and pray. If Jesus Christ Himself took time to prepare, are we to think that we can live victoriously without preparation?

Begin and live the day filled with the Holy Spirit. We are commanded to be filled with the Holy Spirit (Ephesians 5:17-18) and walk in the Spirit (Galatians 5:16-18). As Christians, we possess the Holy Spirit at the time of salvation (Romans 8:8-9). However, we are not always filled with or yielded to the Holy Spirit. Yielding is an act of the will. It is a recognition of the inheritance and power we already have (Philippians 4:13, 1 Peter 1:3-4) and a willingness to live obedient to God's Word and will. We can know if we are filled with the Holy Spirit by our spirit. Our spirit will be characterized by love, joy, peace, long-suffering, kindness, goodness, faithfulness, gentleness, and self-control (Galatians 5:22). Our wisdom will not be self-seeking, but will be pure, peaceable, gentle, willing to yield, full of mercy and good fruits, without partiality, and without hypocrisy (James 3:13-18).

Choose to have a joyful attitude regardless of circumstances. A joyful attitude eliminates most stress! An attitude controlled by circumstances ensures an up-and-down, inconsistent, stressful life and severely damages our relationship with the Lord and witness to others. The Scriptures tell us to be joyful in our trials (James 1:2) and content in our circumstances (Philippians 4:11-13), and to stop grumbling and complaining (Philippians 2:14-15).

Pray without ceasing (1 Thessalonians 5:17). Strong and mature men and women of God are always prayer warriors who are in constant communication with God.

Saturate your mind with God's Word. It is very difficult to stress or confuse a Christian armed with God's truth. We are to hide God's Word in our heart so we will not sin against Him (Psalm 119:9-11). Memorizing Scripture and carrying verses for quick reference is an extremely effective way of minimizing unnecessary stress.

Confess, resist, and run from sin. Unconfessed sin produces stress and guilt. How fortunate

Christians are to have a recourse for sin and to know that although we constantly fail and fall short of the glory of God, we can be cleansed of our sins and all unrighteousness (2 Timothy 2:21-22, 1 John 1:9). In addition to confessing our sins, we are told to resist the devil (James 4:7) and flee from sin (2 Timothy 2:22).

Keep your eyes on Jesus, not your circumstances. Peter was able to walk on water and do all that Jesus could do as long as he kept his focus on Jesus. However, when he focused on his circumstances, he began to sink (Matthew 14:24-33). This principle integrates all of the others. Could it be that understanding this principle is the key not only to managing stress but to a transformed life as well?

Change Your Stress-Producing Circumstances

We should periodically identify, and with the directing of the Holy Spirit, resolve, minimize, or eliminate circumstances that are causing unnecessary stress. Perhaps there are circumstances at work or in your personal life that you could do something about. In Hebrews 12:1-2, we are admonished to lay aside every encumbrance that ensnares us.

Change Your Stress-Producing Behaviors

Since most of our stress is self-created, there is considerable opportunity for reducing stress in this area. Stress-producing behaviors may include, for example, the lack of self-control and self-discipline; disorganization; a lack of motivation and commitment to excellence; procrastination; temperamentalism; unconfessed anger, bitterness, and resentfulness; agitating and self-defeating habits; involvement in sins we won't give up; and most of all, a self-focused and self-serving life.

Christians have an advantage in changing behavior. Change isn't limited to their own efforts. Our job is to know and obey God's Word and will. God's job is to perfect, complete, and transform us (Philippians 1:6). A person with a teachable spirit learns and grows almost daily and continuously eliminates stress-producing behaviors.

Develop an Effective Coping Response Based on Biblical Principles

We can learn a far more effective coping response by developing a stress plan based on biblical principles and practicing the plan until it becomes a habit. There is some evidence that practicing anything, good or bad, for about one month will produce a new habit. Since when we are over-stressed we malfunction mentally, emotionally, physically, and behaviorally, our stress plan should be designed to regain balance and control and turn stress into an opportunity for growth and glorifying God. It is helpful to put your stress plan on an index card and carry it with you everywhere you go. Some ideas for developing a stress plan are:

Know your stress symptoms. (List your symptoms so you will know when you are getting stressed.) Examples are: becoming irritable, touchy, critical, judgmental, temperamental, or angry; anxiety or tension; worry; fatigue; becoming nervous, fidgety, or impatient; defensiveness; attacking others for your problems; aches and pains; self-defeating behaviors; loss of perspective; feeling frustrated or overwhelmed.

Get in mental and emotional balance. Alternatives are: pray and yield to the control of the Holy Spirit; keep your eyes on Jesus and not your circumstances and recall the trials Jesus faced; choose to have a joyful attitude realizing God has a purpose for your trials; confess any sin and resist the temptation to give in to the stress; recall Scripture; think before you act; remove yourself from the situation long enough to get control; gather enough data to accurately assess the situation; choose to process and express your feeling in a mature and constructive way whether you feel like it or not; and seek wise counsel if necessary.

Get in physical balance. Possible alternatives are: take deep breaths to rid yourself of tension; do something relaxing until you are in control; walk, run, exercise; cat nap or rest; listen to harmonious music.

Develop an action plan. Accept the realities of the situation and commit to actions that are consistent with Bible principles. Go through a problem-solving routine (define the problem accurately, gather and evaluate relevant information, explore constructive alternatives, choose the best alternative based on the right thing to do, implement your solution). Accept responsibility for not spreading your stress.

In most cases, it will take only a few minutes to go through your stress plan, although high-stress days may require repeated use.

Manage Your Life
According to Biblical Principles

Stress research conducted by Dr. Don Gardner of the University of Colorado at Colorado Springs and myself clearly indicates that the most effective way to reduce the harmful effects of stress is to have a reasonably balanced life. Balance provides confidence, security, and a sense of worth and control, and enables a person to experience minimal stress even in high-stress situations.

Balance comes from "life management" and is achieved by intuitively or purposefully doing your best to keep balance internally (mentally, emotionally, physically, and spiritually) and externally (continuously prioritizing and balancing the responsibilities and activities in your life such as family, work, finances, service, play, etc.).

There is no simple formula for life management. It is the ultimate challenge in leading a God-directed life. Some basics are:

- live your life solely for the glory of God (Matthew 6:33);
- commit to a life of obedience to God's Word and will;
- make the Scriptures your source of truth for all of life's issues and problems;
- plan your life relying on God's direction (Proverbs 16:9);
- be a good steward of the talents and resources God has allowed you to have;
- do all as a representative of the Lord (Colossians 3:17), committing to excellence (Philippians 1:9-11), running the race to win (1 Corinthians 9:23-27), forgetting past failures (Philippians 3:12-14), and realizing that you are serving the Lord, not man (Colossians 3:23).

Summary

Stress is a major source of victory or defeat in our lives. The way we manage stress and trials is an important spiritual issue. It is a testimony of the genuineness and maturity of our faith and how we see God. Do you see God as all powerful and able to do super-abundantly above anything you ask (Ephesians 3:20), or weak and unable to take care of your stress and trials?

The purpose of trials is to conform us to the image of Christ and draw us closer to God. The key to stress management is to manage stress in the Spirit, not the flesh. Are you willing to manage stress God's way? If so, you can confidently look forward to God turning your trials into opportunities for victory, hope, and blessings.

For Reflection and Action

1. What are some insights you have gained about managing stress from a scriptural perspective?

2. Review the section, "Prepare for the Battles and Challenges of the Day," and make a list of things you would be willing to do to prepare yourself better for managing stress.

3. Identify the stress-producing circumstances in your life that you can and are willing to do something about. Describe what you plan to do to resolve, minimize, or eliminate the stress caused by each.

4. Identify the stress-producing behaviors in your life that you are willing to commit to the Lord for change.

5. Develop a stress plan that includes:

  • your stress symptoms,
  • how you can get in mental and emotional balance,
  • how you can get in physical balance,
  • the action plan you will use for solving problems.

6. Identify ways you can manage your life better and keep it in better balance.

For Meditation

Put the following passage where you will see it several times a day. Read it aloud seven times a day until you have memorized it. Then think about it as you are going about your day, especially when you are in stressful circumstances.

Rejoice in the Lord always. Again I will say, rejoice! Let your gentleness be known to all men. The Lord is at hand. Be anxious for nothing, but in everything by prayer and supplication, with thanksgiving, let your requests be made known to God; and the peace of God, which surpasses all understanding, will guard your hearts and minds through Christ Jesus.

(Philippians 4:4-7)

The *NavPress Booklet Series* includes:

God Cares About Your Work
by Doug Sherman & William Hendricks

Building Your Child's Self-Esteem
by Gary Smalley & John Trent

How to Have a Quiet Time
by Warren & Ruth Myers

**When You Disagree:
Resolving Marital Conflicts**
by Jack & Carole Mayhall

Your Words Can Make a Difference
by Carole Mayhall

You Can Trust God
by Jerry Bridges

How to Know God's Will
by Charles Stanley

How to Overcome Loneliness
by Elisabeth Elliot

**How to Keep Your Head Up
When Your Job's Got You Down**
by Doug Sherman

How to Deal with Anger
by Dr. Larry Crabb

How to Handle Stress
by Don Warrick

Prayer: Beholding God's Glory